Th Peter,
a lot of talk, precious
little cure, but what there
TALKING CURES
is may _be_ precious...

Thanks for being with
me this term at the
New School...it was
encouraging.
Russ Ftrhlt (signature)

RS

10/12/03

Talking Cures

NEW POEMS

Richard Howard

TURTLE POINT PRESS
NEW YORK

Some of these poems have previously appeared elsewhere:

"Odysseys," Raritan, *April 2002;* "Infirmities," Parnassus, *January 2002;*
"The Masters on the Movies," The Yale Review, *April 2002;* "Portrait in Pastel
of the Volunteer Friedrich-August Klaatsch, 1813,"* Literary Imagination, *January 1999;*
"Success," The New Yorker, *January 2001;* "Measure for Measure," Salmagundi,
February 2001; "Further Echoes of the Late Lord Leighton," The Boston Review,
January 2001; "Fallacies of Wonder," Site, *January 2001;* "A Table of Green Fields,"
The Cooper Union, *October 1999;* "The Apotropaist,"* San Francisco Museum
of Modern Art Catalog for Gerhard Richter Exhibition, *October 2002;* "Changes:
Dragon-Flies to Flying Dragons," The Little Theatre of Tom Knechtel, *2002;*
"Close Encounters of Another Kind, Phallacies II," The New Yorker;
"Knowing When To Stop," Salmagundi

For my colleagues in the School of the Arts
(Writing Division), Columbia University

show and tell

CONTENTS

TALKING CURES

Odysseys

A Fugitive

At least in Latin my name wouldn't work
as a *title!* So, better "Ulysses" than the Greek,
    till that novel blew (blackened?) my cover—
what can I call myself now? Each time I try "No Man"
    I feel those fat fingers poking around
for me in the fleece, and I puke all over again!

Where in the world can a man go when each
"immortal verse" is translated into Lapp and Erse
    (and worse)? Everyone knows my history,
complete with goddesses, islands, all those hoary lies!
    I have no tales to tell, I have only
echoes. The real Ulysses puts in his appearance

between other men's lines, the true Odysseus
shows up in unspeakable pauses, the gaps and blanks
    where life hasn't already been turned into

"my" wanderings, "my" homecoming, even "my" dog!
    Start over behind the Old Man's back,
without prowess, fame, or epithets? Not with "my" name(s),

    and someone else's is the one byline
I can't assume. A life to call my own, in the flesh?
    Only when Assigned Readings are over,
only when deathless lines are dust and divine meters
    paralyzed will I be, so to speak, free—
no longer a captive of ballads, bards, and banned books.

    None of them got it right; certainly life,
Latin *or* Greek, bore no resemblance to the Laureate's
    boring (*sic*) lecture, slick as it was . . . To hell
with a crown, a conjugal bed, and recognition
    by a nurse with Alzheimer's! All I want
is to be what I was: mortal, muddled, and myself.

Displaced Person

It was hot and hard going, but worth all
our trouble to find the site:
Agamemnon's Tomb—
the guide was insistent. And who cared
which Agamemnon it was?
The lions were there
above the gate—why not *Mycenae?*
Why not Menelaus too?
So you described it,

returning from a journey to Argos
and eager to set out for
Ithaka next year
to find the True Grave of Odysseus . . .
Don't bother to look. No
archeologist's
trowel, however fastidious,
could raise and rearrange that
cunning skeleton.

*   *   *

Pitch from pine torches has defiled (perhaps
    defended) the sacred cave
      where amorous shades
embraced a living hero's body
    slick with the blood of bullocks.
      Above ground, the sun
rules all surfaces: the reefs, the cliffs,
    even the mud-flats at noon.
      What haven for bones?

Still want to find Odysseus' Grave? Best heed
    the sea's rote and an iron
      keel rotten with salt
clanging on the rocks; second best, read
    several thousand lines of
      interpolated
verse and various lists ascribed to
    a quite imaginary
      rhapsode called Homer.

Another Translator

Phallacies I

Homage to Tante Yvonne

The first one just happened to *be there*, a little like
      Everest or the General's nose
      (remarkable eminences, both)
and also happened to be me, a daunted witness
of that weird Parisian ritual of the Sixties,
      a DeGaulle press conference, summoned
      since I was in Paris at the time
and had been his (or one of his) paraphrasts of prose
concerned with what the General preferred to call (un-
      translatably) *la chose allemande*.

The occasion was particularly rare because
      Mme DeGaulle was at his side and
      (even rarer) willing to answer
questions, provided of course such inquiries observed
the mandates of Presidential privacy. Of course.

But after several anodine
approximations of *politesse*
on the part of the Fourth Estate, a *Herald Tribune*
reporter brought proceedings to a heart-stopping halt:
"What do you regard, Mme DeGaulle,

as the chief significance of life?" And with a sad smile,
after a moment, Yvonne DeGaulle
(whose life had after all included
the death of a soldier son in that same German Thing)
flabbergasted us all by speaking three syllables:
"A penis." And with an interval
of no more than five seconds, a hand
(with perhaps military promptitude) descended
on her shoulder: "I believe the English word you mean,
ma chérie, is pronounced 'Hap-pi-ness.'"

Close Encounters of Another Kind

PHALLACIES II

A dim haunt known as The High Dive
was the scene of my first rapt exposure to
the drawling vowels and the dismissive smile
by which you delivered to outer darkness
    an already blacked-out companion
still decorative enough, despite the toll
of drugs and dirty dancing, to elicit
what seemed, at first, like an indulgent kiss-off:
    No, don't wake him: let lying dogs sleep.

Horrified and charmed by such abuse
(once the point sank in), I knew enough to steer
clear of such tactics as the Freezing Shoulder
and (your words) a Sociable Stab-in-the-Front . . .
    But now you were . . . here! That laugh of yours
could not be missed, even in a triplex flat
(I had my oxymorons down) where gay men
gorgeously dressed (and even gowned) made movement
    —there must have been a hundred of us!—

*   *   *

difficult but quite a lot of fun.
I think the place had belonged to Doris Duke
in the Thirties when The Drive meant Riverside,
or was it Barbara Hutton's hideaway

back then? now come (or coming) to this:
my first *thé dansant*, and with a novice's
nervousness I had to take a piss! I sought
(and found) the proper cubicle for comfort

till I flicked on the light, whereupon

Bingo! right there on top of the tank
appeared a pair of minuscule dragons locked
in coital combat, motionless and *hissing!*
Had I had a foreskin then, it would have shrunk

to string. As it was, what I did have
retracted; I zipped up and quickly withdrew
to join the decorously appareled crew
(though some were already making out,

quite unimpeded by their raiment,

in postures all too reminiscent
of the grappling creatures I so cravenly

left behind)—and found myself now face to face
with you, James Merrill, Terror of the Revels,
        waiting your turn with marked containment.
"Two . . . two lizards in there", I stammered, "fucking
on the toilet tank. They're not moving, but I didn't . . .
I couldn't . . . I don't know how they got there or
        why they're doing that, but you shouldn't . . ."

        And as you glided past me into
the powder-room with the imperturbable
amenity of Talleyrand, you murmured
in the languid accents distinctly recalled
        from that earlier encounter and
reverberating ever since down shared decades
when I would hear them with eager delight, yes,
but always with a touch of fear: *Well of course,
        dear: iguana see, iguana do . . .*

Fallacies of Wonder

September 11, 2001

Most of mind is memory—it is
memory which grants the means of thought.

From modern masters we have learned a lot—
from Freud

> *We remember what we want to remember,*
> *forget what we find no longer important.*

and antithetically from Proust—

> *The only true memory is involuntary.*

but we have yet to learn that memory
is a fallacious mirror, rich but wrong,

useless as record of experience,
for memory IS experience. In the end,

nothing remembered can be true, although
only what is remembered can be real.

*   *   *

Confusion now hath made his masterpiece
and stolen thence the life o' the building.

Often, still, I turn to look downtown
from where I live on Waverly. I trust

the evidence, by daylight or by dark,
of variations in the versions of

those hundred-story towers, so neighborly
I scarcely need to look. I know that I can count

on seeing them where I *remember* them,
no different yet never quite the same.

I do look, though, and, where they were,
replace their being by their absences.

> *Memory can only be artificially improved by the*
> *operation of fantasy towards* ideas *in the Round*
> *Art, which uses magical images, effigies of the stars,*
> *statues of gods and goddesses, or through images*
> *of corporeal things in the Square Art, using buildings*
> *as places.*

*   *   *

Such is the way of wonders: no longer seen
because, being there, remembered merely;

and, no longer there, remembered because
no longer seen. Did they have to be beautiful?

(Was that what the ancient wonders were,
beautiful?) All are gone but the Pyramids—

> *Though palaces and pyramids do slope*
> *Their heads to their foundations, though the treasure*
> *Of Nature's germens tumble all together*
> *Even till destruction sicken, answer me*
> *To what I ask . . .*

merely remembered: gardens, temples, tombs,
a lighthouse and the statues of two gods.

Did some two thousand die for us to call
remembered towers, wonders, beautiful?

> *The reaction has commenced, the human has*
> *made its reflex upon the fiendish; the pulses*

of life begin to beat again; and the re-establishment
of the goings-on of the world we live in make us
profoundly sensible of the awful parenthesis
that had suspended them.

Measure for Measure

Phallacies III

Dear Helen, dear Karl,
until your father died I held my tongue
(though why in *my* English the idiom
for Keeping Still occurs is something of
           an astonishment—
as if that organ,
once let go of, would be liable
to decompose the great speech of silence!)
In any case, I said nothing all through
Kurt's last stages,
           and when the poor man
could bear no more and begged my help to end
his torment, even then I still . . . kept still,
just as I had for all the years he smoked
           more cigars than Freud . . .
"Taciturn Anna",
Kurt croaked from his bed, only half-joking—

it was the name of a child-murderess
when we were students in Prague: a sort of
girl Struwwelpeter.

           Kurt *liked* my silence,
liked it when I merely stared at the cigars
(both of us mindful of their meaning)
and never spoke. Kurt smoked himself away,
           and now I *shall* say
something, if only
to take back silence once you both have heard
an unwonted and perhaps unwanted
but necessary supplement to your
father's history.

           Of course I helped him
to the end he sought—the other silence:
even you, Karl, for all your Principles,
could not object to such a suicide
           as an escape from
advanced lung cancer.
I myself now tend to call it an escape
from something else: *measured penile response
to erotic stimuli* . . . As you know,

Kurt was the doctor
                    who made arousal,
especially "deviant arousal",
a subject for scientific research.
You know that much, and probably you know
                    a little something
more than that as well:
when you were adolescents, quite a lot
of attention (phrased politely enough
to be prurient) was paid to his work
at the Institute:
                    put the offender's
penis in a sealed tube and show him films
of naked boys and/or girls (whatever
the "deviation" may be thought to be);
                    measured displacement
of air from the tube
reveals increases of penile volume,
recorded so the researcher can see
just which images have elicited
the greatest response.
                    Your father maintained

that a child-molester's outlook cannot
be concealed—he was always impatient with
"subjectivity" in psychiatry
and eager to find
verifiable
evidence of these . . . abnormalities.
"The problem is, most men will not tell you
the truth about being attracted to children.
You see, they don't have
much motivation
to say, 'Yes, I did it', or even 'Yes,
I wanted to do it . . .' What we needed
was some device roughly analogous
to lie-detectors,
able to reveal
what a man might not willingly reveal."
By '68, Kurt had perfected most
of his phallometric methods, but
a Communist regime
would not countenance
the research he had begun to develop,
and we "fled"—you were three and five—

from Czechoslovakia to Toronto
         where Kurt continued
testing deviants
at the Institute. By then his cancer
had set in—could there have been some link?—
when he began to recognize in himself
similar responses
         while administering
those "lie-detector" tests he had devised—
symptoms he acknowledged to me, his wife
of forty years, indistinguishable
         from those recorded
phallometrically
in accused molesters of "boys and/or girls".
That was when Kurt decided no longer
to oppose the course of his cancer, though
the means to do so
         were at hand. You see,
my dears, he felt that science had betrayed
him, or else he science. What was science?
The consciousness he now belonged to a
         "community of

sexuality"
came as a maddening revelation.
Such a community, he realized
from the action of his own flesh, could be
                    neither affirmed nor
even disputed
in quantitative terms, and Kurt would accept
no others. The laboratory closed,
the films shown to such "subjects" were destroyed.
You won't remember
                    how such images
had been . . . achieved, such *movies* ever made,
for every care was taken to prevent
the sessions with a boy of seven and
                    a girl under six
from seeming—to them—
a special occasion, memorable
beyond a bathtub full of naked kids.
Their father smoked,
                    and I held my tongue.
When Kurt left us, his means of measuring
penile response was also terminated

—the *first* measurement, I should say. Others
　　　　　have followed his lead
(Bancroft in Akron, specifically)
though employing quite different systems,
as the world knows. No need to speak of this
　　　　　again. Let us all
restore the silence
I have broken somewhat against my will.
I think I have stumbled upon a law
of life: that children must know, at the end,
what their parents know.
　　　　　And so I have told
what I know, as I gave Kurt his release,
and as I put you children in the tub
and trained the camera on your gaiety.
　　　　　For all my silence
I have been the one
to do things, just as I have been the one
to know them. Who would have guessed that but
Kurt, winking from bed at his—and your—
Taciturn Anna.

The Apotropaist

Vielleicht ist da alles sporadisch
—GERHARD RICHTER

On Corfu, a digest of touristic scenery
    after the Meister's own heart
      (as well as his omnivorous art),
    I discovered a temple where the Gorgon
      hung out, tongue out, all

terror and temerity, a Parian mask of
    divine repudiation
      which our Blue Guide to Greece maintained was
    "apotropaic: warding off evils by
      spells, charms, and the like".

True-blue guide to the real right Richter, ever intent
    on a proper closed motif,
      his way of "warding off" to produce
    another ten works at variance, wrecking
      all such intention.

*   *   *

Direct my concentration toward what I do not know
—maddening admonition—
the attempt being to build instead
of burrowing through the undergrowth half-blind
(Richter half-blind!) . . . Yet

what evils the Gorgon can avert are familiar
enough by now: *no systems,*
no program, no ideologies,
no assertion, no purpose, no style! I flee
from all commitment.

Only approximations then, experiments and
inceptions, no end in sight.
Working, for instance, from photographs
of forty-eight dead white masters paralyzed
by the camera,

Richter, being an exemplary monster, destroys
every criteria gained
from his own entrancement, his own
training: *once it's all averted, I can paint*
against my own will.

*   *   *

Letting a thing come rather than creating it—no
          formulations—in a word,
     painting beyond my understanding,
    abstraction an endless becoming,
        endless existing,

space with all the blur of Being on it, *a kind of*
         emergency butchering.
    Does it take the pain out of painting,
   all of this unscrupulously prolific
       production of his?

Repudiating the said in favor of saying
      is all that makes it human,
    this uncertain life of warding off,
  of refusing, this life that is *not the picture*
      but the depicting.

Success

Phallacies IV

Her dealer, who handled successful artists
was a successful dealer,
and his Christmas party, too, was a success:

we all knew it was, for weren't we all there?
And the successful artist
being handled in her eighth decade knew it

too, although she was so old, and had been so
unsuccessful for so long
that she seemed to pay no mind to anyone.

She sat quite still, her rosy scalp glistening
through her rather thin white hair,
and gave no sign of hearing, or ignoring,

any of our successful conversations.
Above the chair she sat in
(like a furnished bone) loomed the decorative

*   *   *

focus of the long room which had been handled
        by a successful designer
of skeletal interiors: a Roman male,

oversize, and barely under overweight,
        every muscle equally
successful—classically nude but not

in the least naked as any man would be.
        And as the talk continued,
Alice Neel leaned back and looked up into

the forking limbs above her head, a pure
        pelvic arch indeed denuded
of the usual embellishment, so that

all that met the eye was a shadowed empty
        socket, the mere embouchure
where once unstinting paraphernalia

must have lodged. "Very fragile things, penises",
        she mused, and for a moment
no one there succeeded in saying a word.

Hanging the Artist

PHALLACIES V

We just can't!—
I trust you realize, Morimura-*san*,
what a powerful and possibly
traumatic impression these pictures of yours are apt
to make on our Houston art-lovers . . . Perhaps
the word is unfamiliar to you—
no, not art-lover, *traumatic*. I must say it is
truly impressive how much English you *have*
managed to learn . . . Of course there will be
some words you haven't had the chance to master, words like
"traumatic"—it means "deeply painful
psychologically". But what *I* mean
is that for our audience, which to this day believes
the camera can't lie, photographs like yours. . . .
No, of course, how *could* there be any
photographs like yours . . . *except* yours? I'm speaking purely
hypothetically, if you know what that means.
Oh, what the hell . . . Your work may cause pain

as well as pleasure. I've tried, as you'll see, to arrange
the show to avoid the unfortunate kind
of misunderstandings that arise
in cases like yours—no, that's not what I mean: there *are*
no cases like yours, really, but provincial
museum-goers (and Houston is
provincial, there can be no doubt about that), even
if they are art-lovers, tend to be repelled
by images that seem to question
or repudiate—you follow me?—the status quo
of gender. It seems to upset people when
standard notions of male and female
are so disoriented—if I may use such a word—
that they are completely fooled, at least at first
glance, and first glance is all most Texans
will spare for what they don't have to pay for . . . Now
you have posed and photographed yourself
with such versimilitude, damn,
so accurately as classic heroines of the screen
in fabled predicaments—oh dear, let's say
in dramatic moments familiar
to us all—not only recognizable but

convincing, that I thought we'd best start with you
     as Kate Hepburn in *Dragon Seed*—
no one could resent something as high-minded and as . . .
     Oriental as the scene you've chosen where
     Peony says, "Come into the garden.
Wan Lung, bring a reed and a bowl of hot water, for
     I am with child". And then we move on
     to the scene in *Of Human Bondage*
where your Bette Davis screams at your Leslie Howard
     (wonderful, how you do them both), "You pity
     me? Well, I pity you, you *cripple*"!
After that, I think your images can make their own
     way in any order you like—Marlene
     and her marvelous coq feathers,
Vivien Leigh in the gown made of green plush portieres,
     Liza Minnelli on that chair in *Cabaret*,
     down to your hallucinatory
(don't bother) version of Marilyn trying in vain
     to gain control over that little white dress.
     I know you sent us *two* Marilyns,
but Morimura-*san*, we *couldn't* show that first one:
     the dress was up to her waist, the girl

was naked, I mean *you* were naked,
and right in the middle of that big black bush of hair
was a prominent penis (I know you know
what *those* words mean). Morimura-*san*,
believe me, the fact that it wasn't a *real* penis
makes no difference whatever. The Houston
Contemporary Art Museum
will not show Marilyn Monroe with a penis, now
Get. That. Straight. How the rest of the show is hung
is open to change. Let me repeat,
I welcome you and your wonderful art to Houston,
though I must remind you that there is a point
of pro-vo-ca-tion beyond which
tradition, and our trustees, will not be moved. I hope
you've understood my English. *Sayonara.*

Changes: Dragon-Flies to Flying Dragons

In the light and the darkness of pictures
by Tom Knechtel

These are seldom seen unless beside the waters
of marshes or fens.
In form they differ little one from another, varying
                              only in color;
all have forked tails, and with these they couple,
for this remaining
motionless some time, evidently giddy in the act
                              of generation.

Of these there is one murderous to bigger others
yet creeping into
an apple, no hole can be seen where he went in:
                              sometimes so tiny
the wonder is, how it were possible that nature
fastens wings and feet
to such minuscule bodies. One somewhat larger
                              has four silver wings

*   *   *

and black eyes flicking out upon two short horns;
it flies ostrich-like,
hopping with the feet, but not for long. And being
                              so greedy for light,
is often consumed in a candle-flame. The female
is nearly alike
but somewhat blacker, and the end of her tail as it were
                              bitten off. Both live

in hedges summertimes, coupling with their tails
twined together, and
so flying, yet sometimes turn again as if to embrace one
                              another . . . Some
of this kind have wings and no feet, some again have
both feet and wings, and
some neither feet nor wings, but are only to be told
                              from common serpents

by a comb on their heads and beard under their cheeks.
Such as these abide
in deep caves and hollow dens, and when they perceive
                              moisture in the air,

come out directly, beating with their wings as it were
with the strokes of oars,
forsaking the earth to fly aloft. Their wings are of
                              a skinny substance

and voluble to a degree, spreading wide according
to the quantity
and largeness of their bodies. The latter are always
                              of sundry colors,
for some are black, some red, some of ashen white,
some yellow even;
and their shape and outward appearance very fearsome
                              to behold, often

with the belly somewhat green, even as chrysoprase
or the spinach jade,
armored to the furthest point by a treble row of teeth
                              upon the two jaws,
and with bright and clear-seeing eyes, usually red,
causing the poets
to feign in their writings that these are the watchful
                              keepers of treasures.

*   *   *

The mouth, especially of the most tameable sort,
is not much bigger
around than a pipe, through which they must breathe,
                                    for they wound not with
their mouth but with the tail only, beating about them
when they are angry.
Yet there is another kind, whereof the teeth, or fangs,
                                    are like to a bear's,

opening wide the mouth and biting deep, wherewithal
they break bones, making
many bruises in the flesh, and of this kind the males
                                    bite even deeper
than the females, yet after this action follows no great
pain upon the wound,
but after such biting there come instead great coldness
                                    and stupidity,

for which cause the place bitten must be washed with
luke-warm vinegar
and an oil drawn out of nettles or sea-onions. Some
                                    when they are hungry

turn themselves to the West and gaping with the very
force of their breathing
draw such birds as are flying overhead into their
                                    throats, which has been thought

but a voluntary lapse of the fowls, to be drawn by
dragon's breath as by
a thing they love, yet surely it is more probable
                                    that some vaporous
and venomous breath is sent up from the beast to them,
whereby their senses
are taken from them and they, astonished, fall down
                                    down into his mouth.

Their age could never yet be certainly known, but it is
conjectured they live
long, and in good health, and therefore grow great.
                              Abiding on land,
some also swim in water, for often they take the sea,
four or five braiding
tails together and holding up their heads, perhaps
                                    seeking richer food.

        *   *   *

Even in our own country have been discovered,
by testimony
of sundry writers, diverse creatures many times seen
                                    flying in the air
at mid-day, and signifying fearful events to follow.
It is even said
there are men who, by certain enchanting verses,
                                    subdue such as these

and ride upon their necks, guiding and governing them
as if on horseback
with a bridle, daily feeding them with their own hands,
                                    and thereafter they
(such monsters) depart having done no harm, though
their footprints remain
perpetual upon the earth. I trust it may be so, yet have
                                    never seen the like.

Colossal

PHALLACIES VI

For close to a thousand years, if you can trust
a patchy Island Chronicle, the harbor
at Rhodes was strewn with huge pieces of bronze;
some, of course, were submerged and are still
there, imperceptibly disintegrating;
you can make them out—is that a shoulder?
perhaps a knee—in certain seasons of the sea,

but most of the seventy-cubit Colossus
(the god Apollo who once guided us well)
lay where it had fallen on stone embankments,
on the beach, on half-sunken ships, their wreckage
a reminder that the statue had been cast
from abandoned armor and bronze weapons
of Macedonians whose siege had failed.

Almost certainly the Chronicle was wrong
or for some advantage of its own had lied

about the arrangement of the Lighthouse God
whose legs bestrid the . . . harbor, offering all
entering vessels an hour-long scrutiny
of the Apollonian scrotum—no doubt
a feature of that Rhodian anchorage.

Now, after a millennium, Apollo
was Ares once more: all the bronze collected
by "Saracen" merchants, shipped to Trebizond
and melted down (again!) for cannon. Not all—
one portion was kept out of the crucibles
by Anna Dalassené, a Byzantine
lady of whom it was frequently observed:

"those cold words 'mine' or 'yours' were never uttered".
It was she who claimed a brazen yard-long chunk
which had first been a spear and was then recast
as the god's phallus. Why the noble Anna
sought and kept the thing is unknown. It vanished
into the Women's Quarters and has been seen
by no man since. So much for the Chronicle.

Another Modest Proposal

PHALLACIES VII

"My students fail", the Eternal Prof complains,
        "to credit the existence of the past",
eliciting copious examples, though
        his indictment's merely endless, not
eternal. For the young, of course, he too
        is history, according to their grim
equation. It is the Prof's existence
        they find it hard to credit. I myself,

a member of the pedagogic caste,
        ambitious to enlist advertence from
precisely those who would withhold it now,
        propose a means of kindling that belief
which "fails", perhaps, to register on minds
        restive in the body's absence or at least
in absence of the body's *language*, words
        acknowledging the presence of the flesh.

*   *   *

Granted the past *is* recalcitrant, still
       close reading, closer *listening* may discern
in recondite sources, suspect archives, odd
       not to say disreputable souvenirs,
such evidences of somatic verve
       our students miss and missing, disbelieve.
Essay, for instance, as a means to crack
       Augustan England's glossy carapace,

this prurience from Walpole's diaries
       purporting to describe the curious plight
of a Marchioness abducted by the Dey
       of Tunis and outrageously content
to fill a favorite's niche in the *harīm* . . .
       Horace gloats: "and now, I understand,
our English rose has roused her busy bee—
       the Lady's happy as the Dey is long".

Portrait in Pastel of the Volunteer
Friedrich-August Klaatsch, 1813

from the catalogue of a German private collection

Little is known about this young Volunteer
depicted in the intricate uniform
of the King's Own Hussars, Second Regiment,
        aside from his dates
of birth (he is fifteen here: Juliet's age)
and death (he will be thirty: Shelley's). Schomberg,
Prussia's leading military historian
        (of course, Schomberg leads—
what else is there for a Prussian military
historian to do, following the Peace
of Tilsit? Anything but follow!), Schomberg
        judges from the height
of the upturned black lamb collar that the boy
must have held the officer's rank of Cornet,
and adds that such gold-braided fur-lined jackets
        were normally worn
over the left shoulder except in winter,

which (to the leading historian) suggests
our soldier's likeness was taken in winter . . .
                    From the catalogue
we learn that Klaatsch has lived half his life. *Aye,*
in the catalogue ye go for men. What if
you were to rest your hand right *there,* barring
                    the gun-metal-gray,
slightly faded sheet with your own living flesh.
Make sure your fingers afford no aperture,
but mask the countenance beneath them so as
                    to conceal those eyes
which even at this remove you find it hard
to meet directly with your own, allowing
yourself by this one gesture to concentrate
                    all your attention
on the other parts of the face, on the mouth
specifically. Suppose you try that now,
lay your hand there (a risky action *in life,*
                    likely to be met
with a drawn sabre and an angry challenge
—though barked in a boy's broken timbre, too loud
for control, the reaction a little too

instantaneous,
revealing that you are not the first to make
such a move upon his person): his reply
to any contact more familiar than some
obligatory
passage of arms between comrades might do you
real damage. No touching, just looking: call it
a kind of military reconnaissance.
Observe, for instance,
the way his hair has been left fashionably
undressed, *à la* Bonaparte, intimating
(surely the right word) our hero has just come
in out of the rain,
or engaged perhaps in some more strenuous
maneuver on a no less fraught battlefield,
that alternative no-man's-land, the bed . . .
Inconceivable!
No lover's hand has preceded your fingers
so eager to smooth those cowlicks or caress
that uneventful skin, those impervious ears:
Narcissus mirrors
your desire with a certain distaste, a certain

contempt—his response will be like those matches
which light only a while after being struck:
                    momentarily
they have forgotten what to do . . . Say you have
masked the eyes, then—escaped the accusation
shining in those agates that a decade hence
                    none of this endures,
nothing survives of the boy except . . . a man
(which survival is the worst breach of faith
in all your idolatry). This being art,
                    not life, do this much:
cover the eyes. The Cornet's other features
offer what his eyes withhold, and you resort,
having parried that icy reproof, to those
                    inviolable
lips in their exemplary conformation;
falling upon them, you may well discover
in the ready pastel flesh, unharassed by
                    that arraigning stare,
the alluring contumely that Heinrich Kleist
was first to honor in his Prince of Homburg,
and Rilke in that fading daguerreotype

of his young father—
the pure sensuality which must depend
on never being known to its possessor,
unsmiling acquiescence which is the whole
seduction of Mars.

Joining

PHALLACIES VIII

No one there would call me "Gisela",
just the name, and let it go at that
as if I was a girl, and if a girl the kind
likely, they said, *to grow one for herself.*
And I had not as yet become "our dear
Dr. Richter" or (God forbid!) "our dear
Dr. Gisela" *who might have grown one*
only to shed the nugatory thing.

In other words, though not exactly old
and not exactly harmless either, I
would be the first woman to be made
(Associate) Curator of Antiquities:
a Marburg doctorate and Germany
in the thirties had made it virtually
a virtue, so to speak, for the Museum
to hire a Jewish woman for the job.

*   *   *

Which did not mean I would have an office
of my own. A desk was found down the hall
from the department (no disadvantage:
there were three windows, and I was away
from the secretaries), so I set to work
and after the first few days began to look
around me. How discouraging to find,
on first inspection, further evidence

I could never belong to the club,
not being one or any of the boys:
ten feet from my desk there was a trunk,
and on the lid a tag: ANTIQUITIES.
MEMBERS ONLY. A month or two went by
and I managed to get up my courage
(*maybe no cock*, I could almost hear them
speculate, *but any amount of balls*)

to open up the thing and look inside,
abashed, appalled, and gratified to find
tray after tray of penises knocked off

how many missing statues, marble, flint,
and granite, some quite obviously plaster
knock-offs of marble, flint, and granite
gone the way of members. I had not been
excluded from the club, just initiated.

Keeping

PHALLACIES IX

Among the friends my mother found it mete,
in her disparagement, to call "kept men";
John H—, like certain secrets, was *best kept*,
till even his unseamed integument
began to verify the poet's verse:
"we are the eyelids of defeated caves".
The time was past all keeping. Johnny aged,
—enough to get himself what mother called

a "real job" (mother never guessed how much
work it took to keep a kept man's life unreal);
he got the best, of course: no longer kept
but keeping—keeping watch over the hoard
of Palazzo Guggenheim, guarded or
maybe given away by Marini's horse
and rider erect on the Grand Canal.

*   *   *

Peggy meanwhile was elsewhere. Having now
a Fafner of her own to mind the art
(how much had she ever minded?) she could
leave town with a clear conscience—to buy more.
Johnny's tale abides, dilemma of
a dedicated chatelain: "My *dear*,
you've no idea what Venetians are,
even visiting types—the temporary

Venetians: thieving magpies, all of them!
Whatever's not nailed down is . . . gone,
and whatever *is* gets pried loose—gone too,
God knows where! I can't imagine *selling*
the objects they contrive to steal—maybe
they just keep them: *ricordi di Venezia*.
What I do know is that every week,
especially when the Biennale's on,

the dong of Marini's horse or the dick
of his happy rider would *disappear*,
broken off for some vile or virtuous
trophy—the one, the other, or the pair!—

to deck what mantelpiece I dare not think . . .
I asked the sculptor to *do something* (he's
from Naples, they know about looting there)
and look what he came up with: these!

which bring to mind my last protector's sleek
hood-mascot on his Rolls, a crystal *chien
phallique*, conveniently removable
—it was Lalique, after all—when cruising
rough neighborhoods, as we were wont to do,
or parking in Parisian *terrains vagues*.
Same principle. Devised, upon request,
for our equestrian *envie de bitte*:

I screw them in to have the Full Effect
(if *she*'s in residence, or Alfred Barr
drops in), *un*screw them when I'm here alone
—I know the drill, although I'm not so sure
which is likelier to befit the horse
and which the horseman . . . Peggy always says,
'Who would notice'? Well, I would, for one,
but that's the difference between life and art".

The Masters on the Movies

NOW, VOYAGER (1942)

Henry James in 1885, the same year he publishes
(serially) The Bostonians

Poor old Boston! Better still, or worse, poor Back Bay!
    Inevitably synonymous with
every cramp and curb and suffocating check
      the flesh is heir to,
    heir*ess* in this instance—Charlotte Vale,
    indentured to a gorgon Ma,

and doomed to be undone by lonely lovelessness:
    happily, here, the *gorgon* turns to stone,
her ugly duckling being metamorphosed
      (medical magic
    and the mystic manipulations
    of modiste and parlour-maid)

to a wandering Wanton of the Caribbean,
    returning as a swan and odorous
with erotic reminiscence to take up

charitable works
in cheerless Boston, for which she has
no likely capacity . . .

The thing is dim to me: Charlotte and her married lover—
what they did and what they should *not* have done;
chiefly there glows for me the figure of
a Changed Woman who
understands when she is spoken to,
a peculiarity

I prize, as I find it more and more rare. For the rest,
on the mild midnight of our actual
screen, I see a phosphorescence, not a flame:
mostly abuse of
voluminous dialogue, absence
of all the other phases

of presentation, so that *line* and *point* are replaced
by a vast formless featherbediness,
billows in which one sinks and is lost. And all
so unrewarding:
it takes us our whole life to learn how
to live at all, and having learned

*   *   *

we die. I make out Charlotte is flexible, as Walt
    enjoins, with all his enviable
  talent for simplifying . . . Be it so!
        Even if, my dear,
    we don't reach the sun, we shall at least
      have been up in a balloon.

LOST HORIZON (1937)

Joseph Conrad in 1907, the year
The Secret Agent *was published.*

Do not be deceived:
  the best of such *songeries* are but trash.
  I hate them, one and all—ineptitudes
  which constitute surely the lowest form
  of amusement, affording nothing more
in the way of *art*
    than a flickering distraction to dolts
    condemned to sit in darkness, mental life
    utterly suspended, watching patterns

of pretence gibber and squeak before them.
A sharp-witted child
can make mere shadowgraphs in pantomime
(Borys has devised a wonderful wolf!)
do more for us than these delusive shades
disporting in an overheated hall . . .
Yet hold! I *have* seen
one movement of a "movie" which has made
sight into Vision, all the blind soul craves:
that moment when a creature who enacts
the Eternal Feminine—Margo? Bargo?
Garbo, it must be!—
becomes before your eyes a ruined hag
once she quits the sacred haunts (lost indeed!)
of a hardly Himalayan Tibet . . .
Instantaneous and incredible
that human matter
could accomplish such disintegration
without passing through long-lasting pangs
of inconceivable agony. Here
was warrant of the long and loathsome dreams
dreamed in the instant
of waking, a whole past life lived with dire

intensity in one last pulse. Yet such
mirages—sudden! slow!—can serve us
only in the incomprehensible
alliance of their
irreconcilable antagonisms,
compelling us to admit what we always
dreaded and denied, that ages of pain
can be lived between two blinks of an eye:
the horizon found!

WOMAN OF THE YEAR (1942)
THE FIRST HEPBURN/TRACY FILM

George Meredith in 1891, the year
The Amazing Marriage *was published*

The shambles, the charnel, the wrinkle—none
of these to be encountered
where the sleekest of amazon daughters
reigns in *superior health,*

* * *

and will reign for some three decades, speaking
    in sentences like scissors,
walking as if born to armor (Woman's gait)
    in a heartbreaker's dozen

of tourneys-to-come, playing opposite
    (opposing) a masculine
adversary—grizzled chin and chiseled grin—
    consternated to be turned,

by the very carapace he employs
    as defense, into a lump
of no account. Soon *she* will learn to live
    out of or inside herself

(it comes to much the same), deprecating
    principle for mere success,
visibly undisturbed by the prospect
    of intellectual value

inseparable from bodily strife!
    Here's an artful pother to rouse
excitement at the several stages
    of their story: catechize

*   *   *

the sacred Laws of the Great Game, lay
    open Secrets of the Hearth . . .
So may the peplum of even the most
    classical goddess be clipped.

Tongue to speak and contend *versus* body
    laid out for probing. Moral:
slack beds make slick battlefields. Since they err,
    imagine they are human.

KING KONG (1933)

Rudyard Kipling in 1894, the year
he publishes The Jungle Book

Once upon a time a Saxon scop
heard of or saw (in those days men commonly saw
    what they wrote about) the ruins of
an old Roman city, half buried and falling
    to pieces in the jungle somewhere
in the south of England. And the tale he made

of his weird discovery—we too
can almost see the band of hunters or raiders
        scrambling through bushes, picking the thorns
out of their legs, standing stock-still in the presence
        of that mysterious dead city—
his saga was my paragon for "The Cold Lairs"
        overrun by a Monkey People.

        Well, I had hoped for something like that,
nothing like the shaky travesty I was shown:
        Denham lost on an "island" where he finds
natives offering Kong their annual maiden . . .
        How could he fail to ask himself: What
happens to those girls? What does the ape do with them?
        Surely Miss Wray herself was aware
of the terrible and transcendental—*sublime*,
        as Burke would have it—experience
of being loved by Kong. Could it be lost on *her*,
        being preferred by a god to all
those consensual black beauties—does it not
        signify the White Woman's Burden?

*   *   *

Even old friend Haggard, he of *She*,
who shares with me the Empire's enemies—would *he*
    so moralize a huckster's conquest?
I scorn the evasion, relieved these failing eyes
    could make out no more than a white rag
fluttering in a black fist. Nor can I believe
    New York was the end, especially
that business (*sic*) of the Dark God's death, falling
    off a skyscraper! For *can* Kong *die?*
'Twas in the jungle that we lost our Simian Lord,
    shambling past some indiscriminate
dinosaurs to true Doom: identity and time
    ever defenseless against Desire.

QUEEN CHRISTINA (1933)

*Willa Cather in 1934, when a second film
version of* A Lost Lady *was set in Chicago, and
Barbara Stanwyck given an affair with an aviator*

Increasingly, conclusively, I am
confirmed in my unalterable choice
(surely it *was* a choice, I do not make
chance decisions) never again to allow
anything of mine   anything I *write*
to be taken away from me and turned
into "material" I have *not* written:
a play, an opera, or (God help us!)
a *screenplay*, as Hollywood proclaims it.

The ultimate wisdom of my resolve
was impressed upon me only tonight,
when a ludicrous account of one more
Roman conversion had me giggling and
horrified: I am   and ever shall be
emulous of the young queen's embracing
a practice so much in accord with her
aspirations (and her accomplishments!),
but the film elided all such matters—

*   *   *

Descartes' friendship, Pascal's dedication
of the just-invented adding-machine
to "Madame la Reine", and above all her
political *astuce* in establishing
her cousin Charles on   the throne of Sweden.
Only Garbo's features were convincing,
and a certain waywardness which I am
tempted to take on faith, despite the terms
of that trumpery *romance*. What stuff!

I suppose it is feckless to look for
anything more from the movies. My own
imaginative knowledge is of loss,
the consequent action of what I write
is of loss as well;   necessarily
whatever celebration I can make
of my experience will be of loss.
Call it poverty who will. There had been
a grain of truth in one moment—the scene

where Garbo (absurd to call that lovely
creature traipsing about in velvet boots

Christina) tries to memorize the room,
running her hands (unforgettable hands!)
over the mantelpiece   and around the walls.
But even Garbo is not worth my words . . .
Leaving the "film palace", I could see
my own breath in the air—numb October
in mournful retreat—and a sickle moon.

Further Echoes of the Late Lord Leighton

Knighted 1878; created Baronet, 1886; created Baron Leighton
of Stretton, 1896; Royal Academician, 1869; President of the
Royal Academy, 1878; Hon. D.C.L., Oxford, 1879; Hon. LL.D.,
Cambridge, 1879; Commander of the Legion of Honour, 1889;
Hon. Member, Berlin Academy, Royal Academy of Vienna,
Royal Academy of Belgium, Academy of St. Luke, Rome;
Academies of Florence, Genoa, Turin, Antwerp; Lieut.-Colonel
of the 20th Middlesex (Artists') Rifle Volunteers.

"Ach, the women! Worse, the wives. And widows worst of all.
Madame Viardot—to hear that I went to Paris. Think
          what she has to overcome:
harsh voice, ugly face, ungainly person, yet contrives
to look almost handsome. Possibly on account of
          Gluck's *Orfeo*, into which
she enters heart and soul. She says it is the only thing
that after fifty performances has given her
          not a moment's *ennui!* No
chance of her singing such in England—I don't believe
a Covent Garden audience would sit through it.
          Speaking of ugly, I am

*   *   *

to illustrate the Evans-Lewes-Eliot woman's
new novel for the *Cornhill*—two 'Florentine' drawings
                for each of the twelve numbers.
Already she writes: 'Romola's face and hair are not
just the thing—how could they be? I meant the hair to fall
                forward from behind the ears—
I shall inevitably be detestable to you . . .' and here
the homely fabulist breaks off with these words: 'Perhaps
                we shall see one another
before you begin the next drawing. My misery
is the certainty I must be often in error'.
                Within the year I have had

analogous nonsense from Browning's wife—*wifely*
nonsense in fact, declaring herself 'satisfied but
                for a want of strength about
the brow, which I must write of, for I can't trust Robert
himself with the message. I think the brow is feeble,
                less massive than his; in fact
your temple is *hollow.* Yet how I thank you for
having put so much of my husband on paper is proved

by the very insolence
of my criticism'. And then another year finds me
designing a slab for the woman in the English
Cemetery at Florence—

talk of hollow temples! Not the faintest what to do
about my title. Father has a place in Shropshire:
Baron Leighton of Stretton
in the County of Shropshire? And the bloody motto?
Swinburne has a way with such things. His way. Advises
Dread Shame. Ambiguous. Well,
why not? And then again, why? What good can come of it?
After the R.A., what price a seat in the Upper House?
Still, the first 'arts' peerage since
Tennyson. That Painting should be lower than Letters
(no higher than baronetcies), inadmissible!
The offer was made. Accept".

The Queen sighed. She could not altogether approve, yet
forty years ago dear Albert had urged the purchase of
Cimabue's Madonna
Carried in Procession through the Streets of Florence—who

could guess what horrors would follow: *The Bath of Psyche!*
                Not even the Prince Consort
foresaw that sea-water of the Lesbian grape could turn
so brackish in the cup. Yet public services weighed,
                and a pure, unmarried life . . .
His last words: "Give my love to the Royal Academy".
The day before his death, the announcement became
                official. The Queen had signed.

Five Communications

STRAYED IN TRANSLATION

April 15, 2002

Gordon S. Nakamura, CEO
Takara-Goldstein Products International,
Osaka. Dear Mr Nakamura:

Two weeks ago I obtained your product dE-BARK
    and attempted to obey the obscure
and for the most part inscrutable instructions

    to the best of my ability. But
even as I struggled to find the meaning of those
    cryptic phrases, I had to ask myself

how Takara-Goldstein hopes to convey canine sense
    if the human version is so abstruse—
admittedly, in translation from a Japanese source.

*   *   *

However, I refused to be daunted
by shaky grammatical constructions (not
 just shaky but actually collapsed)

and some (deliberately?) misleading diagrams:
 arrows pointing nowhere, dotted lines where
mystery prevailed. Of course I persevered,

 but sad to say, have met with No Success
using the device you so confidently propose
 to "puzzled dog-owners". Yet rather

than complain, I prefer offering one or two
 positive suggestions which you may find
helpful in future transactions with your customers.

 It seems to me (and to my husband Tom)
that even though T-G's digital structure is sound,
 the software you are using with it for

bark-recognition leaves a great deal to be desired.
 If I am to explain this criticism
properly, though, I must take a step or two back;
*   *   *

I feel it necessary to describe
the state of affairs—perhaps the "life-style"?—
which led my husband and me to try

dE-BARK. Both of us work (and work on the garden)
at home in rural Connecticut, where
a dog is our sole and assiduous companion;

we have a good deal of acreage and
are likely to be dogged (if you will permit the pun)
from compost-heap to rose-garden by

our hyper-active and really hyper-expressive
brindle Manchester Terrier bitch
(Tom of course insists that we belong to *her*). Indeed

we had to name her Hinda for the way
she obstructs us on all occasions (Tom would add:
for her recurrent costive episodes).

Now Hinda's response to every provocation
is vociferous, both indoors and out,
so of course I assumed a product of the kind

*   *   *

you advertise so plausibly would prove
useful. You claim, based on the signals a dog "emits",
        that this hand-held battery-powered device

will match sounds of all sorts, but especially barks, with
        every digital pattern stored in it,
deciphering even howls, growls, low snarls, and high yelps

        as six "feelings": *self-expression, alarm,*
and *frustration,* then *appetite, sadness,* and *desire.*
        Well, such generalities may apply

to Japanese dogs, or even to dogs in Japan,
        but constant intercourse with Hinda
has convinced me that you have not calibrated

        your product's program with appropriate
(not to say accurate) translations. For example,
        for one type of bark your device displays

as pertinent words: *How Boring.* Now I ask you,
        dear Mr. Nakamura, could even
the most cursory attention paid to barking dogs
*   *   *

qualify these words as *self-expression*?
Long experience affords me a much likelier
     rendering: *I Don't Know Why I'm Barking!*

a frequent canine expression any dog-owner
     will recognize as universal, though
as a matter of fact, there are no universals in

     the world of canine feelings, or elsewhere,
I suspect; barking, like human speech, refers to
     specific instances, special incidents.

What dE-BARK regards, for example, as *frustration*
     or in some diapasons as *desire*
had much better be rendered as: *Oh, There Goes a Cat!*

     It is far from my intention, of course,
to replace your entire program of digital
     patterning with our Hinda's lexicon;

I wish merely to suggest, having got nowhere with
     the present software of dE-BARK's program,
the possibility of a more reliable
*   *   *

language-version of barking behavior.
You will, I am sure, concur (and indeed, to digress
    for a moment, might not ConCUR provide

a wider concept and a somewhat catchier name
    for your product whatever the final
form a revised version of it might take? Just a thought!)

    —concur that *sadness* is more tellingly
recast as the human phrasing of original
    canine sentiment by an outcry

or outburst something like: *Oh, the Cat's Getting Away!*
    and that such a nebulous notion as
appetite is much more clearly focused by the words:

    Drop That, Drop That: I'll Eat It!
Furthermore, drama plays such an inveterate
    role in a dog's life that it seems almost

a betrayal of trust to let such a tired word as
    alarm represent what barking conveys
in actuality: *You Don't Belong Here: Get Out!*

*   *   *

I offer such interpretations as
no more than a start, Mr. Nakamura, but a start
    based on close and continuous study

of the canine idiom it is T-G's declared
    mandate to transform into human terms.
Though I am disappointed by dE-BARK's present-day

    performance, I know real improvements lie
within reach, of that I am certain, and it would be
    a privilege as well as a pleasure

to have some small share in their realization,
    if you find that my recommendations
(I have others, of course) possess sufficient merit.

    Should further consultation be desired,
I (and my husband of course, not to mention Hinda)
    will be delighted to hear from you or

perhaps from some more specialized member of your staff.
    Meanwhile, since we should like you to regard
us as your colleagues—collaborators or at least

*   *   *

confederates in progress—you must not
dream of refunding the $104
    which dE-BARK costs in the United States

(as you surely know in your capacity as
    T-G's Chief Executive Officer).
Faithfully yours,
                Annabelle (Mrs. Thomas) Eden

Two Ways to Skin a Catalogue

April 27, 2002

Mrs. Thomas Eden and Family
Wewauka Brook, Bridgewater, Connecticut
    Dear Mrs. Eden, My superior,

Mr. Nakamura, has assigned me the honor
    of replying to your recent letter.
What you have to say is of great interest to us, for
*   *   *

Takara-Goldstein International
is always concerned to improve the products offered
to our customers, and in those cases

where amelioration is impossible, we hope
to afford satisfaction in other
areas. Please find enclosed our check to the amount

of $104 (Company
Policy, alas, forbids refunding postage for
unsolicited communications),

along with our sincerest regret that you have been
disappointed with the performance of
dE-BARK, which is of course the most recent

item in our extensive catalogue
(which I enclose as well) of gear designed for dogs and
dog-lovers. dE-BARK is in fact so new

that yours is the first comment sent from our customers
abroad. Our Japanese clients, meanwhile,
continue expressing the most enthusiastic reactions,
*   *   *

and I venture to suggest, Mrs. Eden,
that a certain national, perhaps even racial
    discrepancy accounts for the problem

you mention with regard to dE-BARK's six translations;
    a certain native restraint, I believe,
is answerable for the abstractions you deplore

    in the "messages" your dE-BARK presents.
I do not mean that Japanese pets are more repressed
    than Manchester Terriers or than any

other dogs owned by Americans (which must include
    some of our Japanese breeds, after all),
but merely that our versions of canine expression

    (as manifested in dE-BARK's software)
are more likely than not to be generated by
    the Japanese mode of organizing

any and all evidence of affective conduct
    into group compulsions, group essentials . . .
And I should guess, Mrs. Eden, that your decoding
*   *   *

of Hinda's barks is to a like degree
the characteristic consequence of your own
        civil endowment, the American Way

of prizing comportment precisely as it appears
        to be individual. These are merely
speculations, of course, but until we have further

        confirmation from customers abroad,
we cannot modify our software, I am sorry
        to say, in accord with your suggestions;

in the meantime, on behalf of Takara-Goldstein,
        please accept Mr. Nakamura's and
my own best wishes for the happiness of your whole

        family—I include Hinda, of course—
and our admiration for your acute discernment
        of the dog's actual meanings expressed

in her barking, however improperly you find
        dE-BARK has construed them. Yours, M. Ito,
First Vice-President in Charge of Public Relations.

In-House Memo

Re: Eden complaint.
From: M. Ito *To:* G. Nakamura Gordon darling,
       this will have to do. I am hindered

(irresistible word!) from functioning more cogently
       for you by my personal conviction
the impossible woman is absolutely right.

       I know, I know: according to the line
I've handed her, the Japanese, even Japanese Vice-
       Presidents, don't want to have personal

anythings. Please forgive me for resorting to
       all that collective Shinto bullshit—
it's hard to make much of a case when you're convinced

       otherwise. You know damn well how the dogs
react when you honor me by spending the night:
       Tina barks and Turner growls, and that's not

self-expression, that's *You're lying in our bed: now leave!*
       Maybe they don't beg the way Hinda does
(terriers are so abject), but you yourself told me

*   *   *

  my griffons were saying: *Give us that fugu,*
we'll risk it! There's Samurai virtue! And I suspect
   you like the way Samurai virtue ends . . .

Once they get outside, we both know they're insisting:
   Get us that kitty, we need that kitty! . . .
Well, it's too late to revise dE-BARK for the Edens,

  but what if we started on a reverse
software—you know, translating the right remarks
   into how dogs put it . . . M-BARK, maybe?

Meet me at the Red Setter after six, and we'll try
   some digital structures that might keep
Tina *and* Turner off the bed with a few telling

  barks. (Bet we could sell *that* to Annabelle!)
Are you game? From the bottom of my (collective) heart
   I remain your (singular) Masako.

REASSURANCE

June 1, 2002

Dear Miss Ito—as I know you to be,
    for although you signed
yourself with no more than a genderless initial,
    a mere glance at the impressive column
        of vice-presidents
down the left side of Takara-Goldstein's equally
    impressive stationery was enough
        to enable me
to make out your given name as well, and after that
    a few moments of research on the web
        (how persevering
I can be you must already realize) sufficed
    to make manifest that in Japanese
        the onomastics
of "Misako" are invariably feminine—
    though it must be said that if I could decode
        the instruction-sheet
for dE-BARK, such deductions were "elementary,

my dear Miss Ito", as Holmes might put it—
    thank you very much
for your letter, the supererogatory check,
    and the catalogue. It is the latter
      which concerns me now,
though I do admire what you call your *speculations*;
    I believe you've put your finger on some
      characteristic
and crucial divisions in our national *mores*;
    I don't in fact consider myself a
      representative
American, any more than you, dear Miss Ito,
    would choose to pass for a typical
      Japanese woman
(though I could be mistaken about this assumption,
    for that initial M of yours might well
      express what you have
identified as a "group compulsion"). But really,
    don't all of us like to think of ourselves
      as exceptional?
Even Hinda does, as I was getting round to saying,
    and that is why I am now ordering

item 19V

from your intriguing catalogue (my check is enclosed).

Unlike dE-BARK, which had to translate

canine expression

into human terms not only approximate but,

as I was obliged to discover, quite

fallacious, "FLEECE-BOY"

strikes me as entirely capable of conveying

human meanings accurately to dogs.

Though once again, dear

Miss Ito, I must point out that the prose employed to

describe some items in your catalogue

is virtually

perverse in its ambiguity (when it is not

downright misleading), but

if I correctly

understand the curious text accompanying

the photograph—of an adorable

Akita (it is

an Akita, isn't it?) with FLEECE-BOY in its mouth?—

one's own dog, when home alone and lonely,

would similarly

resort to FLEECE-BOY for comfort? Whereupon, nestled
      inside the toy, a recordable chip would
           be activated
to communicate with the dog *in my own voice?*
      So that each time we had to leave Hinda
           I could re-record
the identical chip with whatever message might
      seem appropriate for the occasion—
           have I got that right?
I certainly hope so, for FLEECE-BOY (if this is indeed
      what he can do) sounds like the answer to
           our difficulties:
as I believe I mentioned in my earlier letter
      Hinda, though at six hardly a puppy,
           is hyper-active
and when left alone tends to demolish anything
      she can find to chew up around the house.
           You will understand,
therefore, and perhaps even sympathize with our zeal
      to leave a first message for Hinda;
           I am confident
that if I can leave a chip inside FLEECE-BOY saying

in a voice the dog actually *knows*,
      "Don't Do That, Hinda!
Good Dog! We'll Be Home Soon", my husband and I
      might look forward, on those occasions when
          both of us must be
away, to a less chaotic household situation
      thanks to FLEECE-BOY, Takara-Goldstein and
          most of all to you,
dear Miss Ito, with our warmest greetings as well,
                         Yours,

      Annabel (Mrs. Thomas) Eden and
      unquestionably
Hinda. My husband has some ideas of his own
      concerning FLEECE-BOY as well as dE-BARK
      and tells me he will
be in touch with you and/or Mr. Nakamura
      independently (which sounds ominous
      but I am certain
his points, whatever they are, will be of interest).
      Again, my appreciation for all
      you have done. A.E.

THE APODOSIS

June 20, 2002

Dear Miss Ito: My wife Annabelle, from whom
        you received, in recent months,
two letters, I think, as well as orders for

        items manufactured by
your employers, has given me your name
        and Mr. Nakamura's,

though not the correspondence—she insists
        confidentiality
must prevail between purveyor and purchaser.

        I proceed, consequently,
at a certain disadvantage, though hardly
        for the first time (there have been

similar occasions, I can assure you),
        with my appeal, though perhaps
the more trenchantly for that very reason . . .

*   *   *

Please do not accept further
occasions for correspondence with my wife,
        however advantageous

such communications may appear to your
        firm's commercial interests.
To do so would only encourage her in

        the singular delusion
which from time to time besets her existence,
        though when not provoked by these . . .

occasions, intermitting almost wholly
        (I assume you have observed
how coherent and indeed how eloquent

        Annabelle can be, even
in the grip of her obsession, or perhaps
        especially under such

circumstances). Not since 1968,
        when Hinda was run over
in the driveway, before our very eyes,
*   *   *

have we had a dog. But when,
by an inopportune circumstance, my wife
hears of some device likely

to rouse those fond associations of hers,
she regresses (or perhaps
it is really a sort of forward impulse)

to the days when poor Hinda
was our problem and of course our pride as well;
in consequence we acquire

a good many (rather expensive) items
which serve no purpose except
to distress my wife (who refuses, of course,

to allow me to purchase
another dog of any breed whatever).
Therefore I must implore you,

Miss Ito, whatever the provocation,
not to respond to any
further inquiries or orders for purchase

*   *   *

from my wife. Your compliance
will return our household, I have no doubt, to
        its wonted train of events

and restore Annabelle to herself once more,
        an identity for which
you have my heartfelt thanks, even in advance.

        Please extend my gratitude
to Mr. Nakamura who I believe
        played some part in the drama

of this distressing phantasmagoria.
        In hopes of recovery
I remain,
        yours very truly,
                Tom Eden

A Table of Green Fields:
Richard Upton's Cortona Landscapes

My intention to forget was neither
a success nor a failure. Only Freud,
in 1899, would acknowledge
            such an "intention",
but in the century since, forgetting
(proper names above all—"Signorelli"
in Freud's case) has tended to become
            as canonical
in our catalogue of commendation
as remembering ever was: sometimes
we leave out *because* we love. In my case—
            in Cortona once,
searching for a "lost" Signorelli locked
in the Duomo sacristy, I stood
—I must have stood—in this same piazza
            rapt by these very
viridescences closing in, opening
out—yet forgotten forty years, forsworn,

forsaken for the sake of getting on
     with mere life, yielding
to attritions of travel, erasures of
whatever came next (the next best thing) . . .
When out of the blue—no, the *green* of what
     let's call Upton's Rise
or Resurrection (tireless little webs
that ring the town like working vertebrae
and tend to do their work without a sky)
     there came back to me,
came *forth* to me, not just "I know the place!",
not even "I was here!", but in the paint
the memory (as if by madeleine):
     "this is my body!"
We have art so we may not perish from truth.
Now probably Nietzsche meant more by that
dark saying than my recapture of some
     green forgotten hills,
more than my learning, as I claim to have
learned from Upton's Rise, how a landscape lives
in me as I would live in it. Yet an order
     of form suffices:

like Freud's, my intention to forget
was neither a failure nor a success,
seeing as how, in Cortona, I managed
        to unearth a sketch
of the celebrated *Resurrection*
of the Flesh that Signorelli frescoed
on the walls of God's great black-and-white barn
        in Orvieto.
But found in Upton's painting "off the wall"
what I'd forgotten (what I'd intended
to forget?) half my life: Resurrection
        of the Earth in me.

Infirmities

No use having an executor, Horace Traubel,
       literary or the other kind
unless I can show you what to execute.
Losing every damn thing all over again, Horace.
       I need you: this floor's become a *flood*—
dive in! See if you can't come up with something:
letters—tied in green ribbon—from an "Abraham Stoker."
       Wrote to me from Dublin, years ago . . .
Now he's coming to see me, or to let me
have a look at him. Either way, I must lay hands on
       those letters . . . I know they're here somewhere.
Mary Davis is no help at all. Once a week
she comes to clean house, that's what she calls it, forages
       through my mail as if it was haystacks—
only thing she could find down there's a needle!
No, in *that* pile, Horace . . . Letters from the Seventies:
       I recall the first one came as if
for my birthday—fifty . . . long past now. Some things
you don't forget. Keep looking, Horace: a young man's hand,

twenty, he said . . . Middle-aged by now
(I thought so at forty, know better today.)
That's it! the green ribbon—green never fades. I chose it
for Ireland. Just read out the top one,
then you'll understand why I kept the others.

Put this letter in the fire, if you like,
but so you do, you'll miss the pleasure of
this next sentence, which ought to be that you
have defeated an unworthy impulse:
You are a true man, Walt, as I would be
myself, & therefore I would be to you
as an apprentice is to his master.
You have shaken off the shackles, therefore
your wings are free. I wear the shackles still
on my shoulders, tight—hence I have no wings.
I write to you today because you are
different from other men. If you were
the same as they, I would not dare to write.
As it is, I must either call you Walt
or not name you at all—I have chosen
the better course. I thank you for the love

& sympathy you've given in common
with my kind . . . I have read your poems, Walt,
aloud to myself with my door locked
late at night, & read them on the seashore
where I could look round me & see no more
sign of human life than ships out at sea,
& there I often found myself waking
from a dream with the book lying open
beside me . . .

". . . on the grass . . ." Stop, Horace. I remember what comes next,
            and I need to hear it, too. But first
      what *you* need: this Stoker fellow's here! Coming
today to Mickle Street. Now when he rings, you let him
            in, Horace, then leave us two alone.
      Stoker thought he was writing to me, of course,
but it was really to himself. I answered—warmly,
            I always do, to the personal.
      I wrote with my whole heart. Now read me some more.

   . . . If I lie out on the grass,
those days come back to me with undying
freshness. I look among the stalks or blades

& wonder where the energy comes from—
that fond hum of Nature, never ceasing,
for ears that can hear. I guess at what is
below the brown uneven earth that seems
so level at a distance, so rugged
in reality. At such moments comes
the wisdom of those half-forgotten thoughts,
the rudiments of all philosophy . . .

That boy was my reader, no doubt about it. We need
       our readers, every one. Now we'll see
   what this man's done with that boy. Today's letter—
oh, I can manage to find a letter that comes today,
      Horace: today is easy to find;
    it's yesterday I tend to lose . . . Stoker writes
different from the way he used to. Guess we all do that.
      Sorry to have lost what was in his
    early messages. Lord, what I've lost in mine!
He sounds polite enough now, of course, but determined
      to settle the business of the day.
    Explains he's come over here with Sir Henry
Irving, Irving the actor—they knight them over there—
      manages the Lyceum theater

for him in London, brings the whole troupe
here on tour. Says "Sir Henry" has contracted to play
            New York, Philadelphia, Washington . . .
      I played Washington, in a manner of speaking,
before Washington played me—played me out! . . . Stoker has
            his reasons for coming today, says
      he needs me—needs me *again* is what he says.
Maybe so. You let him in, Horace, send him up here
            to me, and if he don't come back down
      in half an hour, you collect him. Half an hour's
all I can stand of any man's "needing"—even mine!
            Now read some more young Stoker, till
      the old one gets here.

I know about the grass because for years
I could not walk, though no one ever put
defining names to the disease I had.
Certainly till I was about seven
I never knew what it was to stand upright.
But I was naturally thoughtful, &
the leisure of long illness gave the chance
for fruitful thoughts later on: healthy ones.

All my early recollections are of
being carried about in people's arms
& of being set somewhere or other—
on a bed or sofa, if in the house,
or if the weather was fine, on a rug
outdoors, or even right out on the grass . . .

. . . There's the bell! Stop right there—
"on the grass", of course. I know the sound of my own bell:
One thing I still recognize. All right,
let that be your signal, Horace. Go downstairs,
let him in, send him up. We may have something to say
to one another . . .
Welcome, Stoker—
welcome, Abraham! Let's greet one another
as old friends, as indeed we are . . .

Sir, I cherish your friendship, but the name
a friend must know me by is changed: it's Bram,
Bram Stoker *I call myself, sign myself,*
now that I endeavor to write . . . fiction.

*   *   *

I overlook the change
of name—dislike it, actually.
Stoker was born Abraham, and he should be
Abraham still—has the breath of humanity in it,
and Lincoln too. Can't "Abraham" write
fiction as well?

Surely you'll sanction the change, Sir: you too
must have known a like need for a new name.
Were you not called "Walter" before the Leaves?

You show an old man his place . . .
Glad to be there. The years might have blurred that need. The man
Stoker repeats, no—fulfills the boy!
You took a shine to me over in Ireland,
when you were at Trinity. I value your good will:
maybe you've remained of the same mind,
in substance, as at first . . . You see, I prepared
myself for your visit by reading those old letters
of yours. Appears from what you wrote me,
if I understand you rightly, that we share
infirmities. Most men do, of course. Sometimes I think
it's all they share. All they *can* share. But

our weaknesses, yours and mine, set in
at opposite ends of life: old age has withered me,
              nowadays they put me out to grass
        on a blanket, just as you lay there in your
own childhood. The grass is the same—for you in your first,
              for me in my second, most likely.
        Still and all, I get up, get dressed, get outside
most days. Live here lonesome enough, but in good spirits . . .
              You find me . . . Well, how do you find me?

> *I'm honored, sir, by your welcome, and*
> *happy you still recall the impetuous*
> *and perhaps importunate outpourings*
> *of a faltering youth to Walt Whitman*
> *many years ago. That makes it easier*
> *to come to you with my questions again.*
> *I would not tax your strength for all the world,*
> *and my own duties—surely I explained*
> *that my obligations to Sir Henry*
> *will not permit me to trouble you long*
> *—there was, in fact, some difficulty*
> *finding my way to Camden and to you—*

but I'm gratified to be here at last.
How do I find you, sir? I find you just
as I hoped you would be: that wonderful
mane of white hair over your collar, that
munificent moustache over your mouth,
to mingle with the mass of flowing beard—
you know, you are rather like Tennyson.
You quite remind me of him as he was
at the Lyceum—you don't mind that, do you?

Mind! I like it! Why, I'm proud to be told so.
I like being tickled! Irish flattery is best—
    found that out when Mr. Wilde was here,
  had all the sauce an old stomach could swallow.
Still, what a broth of a boy he was! Younger than you,
    I guess—you ever know him, back home?

I knew his mother, Lady Wilde. She kept
a sort of salon in Merrion Square—
in fact it was there I first met my wife,
one of those Saturday at-homes. Florence
—that's my wife—was a friend of Oscar's too . . .

*   *   *

Hah! You're married, and respectable,
and an author of "fiction" into the bargain . . . Not
often such a man comes to me with
questions. Young Wilde asked some—a *salon,* you say?
That explains a lot. All about art they were, art with
a big A. I spell it small, myself . . .
If you haven't much time, put your questions, son,
but let me get mine in first. What sort of fiction is it
that you must "endeavor" to write?

Well, usually I dash things off, not
much more than typed-up drafts, to pay debts,
you know, or to earn some extra cash. But
lately I seem to have come once again
under your spell, sir: I too have a sort
of poem I must write—oh, it's in prose,
of course, but you understand that—and
there are characters to speak the lines, and
in a sense they revolve around one man
who rather resembles you, sir. He too

has long white hair and a heavy moustache,
powerful bearing, something . . . leonine.
He too longs to pass through the crowded streets
of mighty cities, to be in the rush
of humanity, to share life, change, death—
all that makes us what we are. Is this not
Walt Whitman's "call in the midst of the crowd"?

I don't know that it is. Tell me some more, "Bram",
let me hear what you want to do with me . . . *Leonine*?

Yes, masterful. You know: the king of beasts.
I've written quite a lot about the man
modeled on you. In my narrative,
all others serve him, or come to do so . . .
I can even recite for you the way
Count Dracula (that is my hero's name)
is addressed by one of his followers
when the Count is introduced: "I am here
to do your bidding, Master, I am yours,
and you will reward me, for I shall be
faithful. I have worshipped you long and far.

Now that you are near, I await commands,
and you will not pass over me, will you,
dear Master, in your distribution of
all the good things that are within your gift? . . ."

I don't much like this talk of Masters
and Counts. What is it he's done, this Dracula,
that everyone is so eager to serve him? Does he serve
others in return?

It was you, sir, who gave me the clue, you
who spoke of adhesiveness, that union
beyond any binding together of bodies,
a universal solvent in the blood . . .
I found it in Leaves of Grass *long ago,*
and to what I found have tried to be true.
It was your own poem, your own words
which guided me, and which will guide me still.
Surely you will remember "Trickle Drops" *. . . ?*

Make it a rule
that if I wrote it, I don't remember it.

The *Leaves* is not a sacred book, but a growing thing.
    The text is in a state of constant
    transformation. To see what I've changed *from* what
to what, Horace keeps the old book here—you find the poem,
        Abraham, read it to me yourself,
    then maybe I can link my lines to your Count . . .

> *The privilege of reading Whitman's words*
> *to Whitman's ears is beyond presumption . . .*
> *Here it is, in "Calamus", the teaching*
> *I have tried to make into a tale . . .*

Oh, in "Calamus" is it? Then I don't wonder. That
        was what they wanted me to cut out.
    All the English critics urged me to it: "Your book",
they said, "will go into every house in America.
        Surely that is worth the sacrifice"?
    It would not be any sacrifice. So far
as I care, they might cut a thousand. It is not that—
        it is quite another matter. When
    I wrote as I did, I thought I was doing
right, and right makes for good. I think that all God made is for

good, that the work of His hands is clean
in all ways, if used as He intended. No,
I shall never cut a line so long as I live. Read
          me the news from naughty "Calamus".

"Trickle drops! my blue veins leaving!
O drops of me! trickle, slow drops,
Candid from me falling, drip, bleeding drops,
From my face, from my forehead and lips,
From my breast, from within where I was conceal'd,
          press forth, red drops, confession drops,
Stain every page, stain every song I sing, every word
          I say, bloody drops,
Let them know your scarlet heat, let them glisten,
Saturate them with yourself all ashamed and wet,
Glow upon all I have written or shall write, bleeding drops,
Let it all be seen in your light, blushing drops".

Yes, that's right: we put that in ahead of
"City of Orgies". I mind that well—the same fool English
          said it was "a pity not to cut
          certain passages", and I knew just the ones:

"Trickle Drops", then the lines that come at the end of
          "City of Orgies": ". . . These repay me,
     lovers, continual lovers, only repay me".

     Then you follow me, sir, as I do you . . .
     to the point where the Count dismisses
     the Vampire Women to claim the bleeding
     youth for his own: "This man belongs to me".

          "Vampire Women"? No such thing.
     And is your Count a vampire too? Inspired
by Walt Whitman and a *bloodsucker*?

     I want to make the voluptuousness
     of death equal to the deathlike nature
     of love. Like you, sir, I dare my readers
     to acknowledge that the mystery of
     sexual love is worth dying for . . .

                    . . . Not "like me", Stoker!
     Only worth *living* for, that's *my* mystery,
if you can call it such. Take your Count back home with you,
          let Sir Henry have him. I've heard of
     his ways. Heard how they're going to settle

the Bacon-Shakespeare dispute . . . Going to dig up
      Shakespeare and dig up Bacon, then let
   Sir Henry recite *Hamlet* to them. And the one
who turns over in his grave will be the author! Heard
      that one, have you, Abraham Stoker?

> *Frequently, sir. And many others too,*
> *in all the years of my service. You see,*
> *I am indentured to Henry Irving*
> *in the same way I once tethered myself*
> *to you. By doing so, perhaps in both*
> *servitudes, I've learned that close relations*
> *between two people, any two, always*
> *afford vampiric exploitation. Sir,*
> *I fear you find my expressions . . . misplaced:*
> *no one, I now perceive, may pluck the heart*
> *out of Walt Whitman's mystery, who lives*
> *according to the Eleventh Commandment*
> *of Modern Times . . .*

As if ten weren't enough. I don't hold much with
commandments, Abraham. What in Hell's the eleventh?

*   *   *

"Thou Shalt Not Be Found Out".

That's one I'll obey . . . Abraham, here's
Horace, he'll take you to the Mickle Street car:
you're sure to find your way with him . . .
Goodbye, son, there's no
bad blood between us now, am I right?
Please to give my best regards to Mr. Wilde,
when you see him next . . . Another fine Irish (whisper this)
man of art. Endeavor to write your
own fiction, young fellow. Good fortune with it.
Nothing to do with me . . .

Good-night, Horace. Leave a lamp.

Knowing When To Stop

October, 1939

...*D*estroy the dogs, Highness?
Where did you ever get such an idea?
That's not our British way. It sounds more like
some primitive practice than anything
          appropriate to
the death of a modern public figure.
You know the kind of thing I mean: Siegfried
or Sardanapalus—the perished hero
          laid out on a pyre
surrounded by his wives, his dogs, his things,
all to be done away with, given to
the flames along with his defeated flesh.
          Who could imagine
anything like that in London today?
Your Highness will never experience
such barbarism here in Primrose Hill,
          on that I give you

my word of honor as an English vet
—than which, I venture to say, there can be,
in such a case, no firmer guarantee:

we don't do such things!

Of course we don't, dear Dr. Gravesend, not
any longer. But may I remind you
even so (speaking as a foreigner)
such things have been done.
And having done things, just the once, becomes
a ruinous reason for doing them
again, even after so long
an interruption.
Perhaps the notion you did away with
the dogs is a primitive atavism
of mine. You see, for us Professor Freud
was our patriarch,
a kind of tribal hero, gone although
never truly absent. It was because . . .
Did you know—how could you know?—it was I
who gave him the chows,
first Jofi, then Lün. For Jews in his day,

such creatures were not, as they are for us,
(for me, at least) erotic household gods—
            vermin more likely,
I had to laugh when my old friend would say:
"Dogs love their friends and bite their enemies,
quite unlike people, who are incapable
            of pure love and hate
in their object relations". They were his
companions to the end, almost the end . . .
You probably know what happened then,
            if you were sent for . . .

No, Princess. I knew (it was all I knew)
that nothing could keep the Professor from
his visits to the quarantine kennels
            here at Ladbrook Grove.
He crossed London every week to see Lün—
played with her, talked to her for an hour.
I myself had done the operation
            (ovarian cysts)
on Jofi, so I could see for myself
how moved he was by her sympathy

during his own surgery: "as if she
        fathomed everything",
he kept saying, "One wonders when one will
get used to it. But of course one cannot
easily recover from seven years
        of intimacy . . ."

Oh, the Professor and those "one's" of his!
All the same, "one" brought Jofi to Paris
—it can't have been an easy maneuver—
        and on to London
where you operated on her cysts,
and "one" saw Lün through quarantine as well,
an then they were with "one" for good, or so
        we thought, till the days
of the last operations when putrid
secondary infections ate a hole
in the Professor's cheek. The smell of which
        drove away the chows.

Now that's . . . I must confess I am surprised
to hear his dogs forsook the Professor.

No one mentioned that when I was sent for—
>*not to destroy them.*
Princess—to take them back to Ladbrook Grove.
We found a home for Lün; Jofi's still here,
you may see her whenever you please, though
>*she's too old to be*
placed with strangers now. I can't help thinking
how peculiar it is, the Professor
being abandoned, rejected by his
>*own dogs at the end . . .*

>That was how he knew it must be the end.
>When the dogs no longer came to his bed
>but stood beside the door—not cowering yet
>>not allowing him
>to touch them—the Professor no longer
>refused sedation: "Now it is nothing
>but torture, and makes no sense any more.
>>Remember our pact".
>So Doctor Schur gave him the morphine then,
>and later that night our Professor died.
>Surely you can understand my seeing

something heroic
in the whole occasion, perhaps something
primitive, as you say, something even
barbaric about consenting to death
when love is denied,
yet something befitting these times when
so much is taken away, so much lost . . .
You know, I don't believe I feel much need
to visit Jofi . . .
Better to leave the poor old girl in peace—
she's had a dog's life. That's one difference
between us and them, doctor: stench or no
stench, I hope I'd have
sufficient piety if not "pure love
and hate in object relations" to kiss
my master farewell.